TO WHOM IT MAY CONCERN

Part 1

Stephanie
Oderoha

ISBN: 979-8-9866396-0-4

Cover art by Tyinkwell

Contents

Acknowledgements

First I would like to thank God for placing these testimonies in my life to share with the world. I wrote this book out of obedience. I believe God said that now is the time to share my life with you all. I've never had a hard time sharing when I saw fit but this is quite different from that. This is about transparency and healing. Healing for those who could never find the words that gave adequate justice to their misfortunes. This is about laughter. You really do have to laugh at your pain sometimes, because the audacity is worth cracking up over when you look back. This is about release. Letting go of things and people that failed us and embracing the plans God has for us. I thank my mom for being such a supportive force in my life. I thank my sister for also being an amazing support system for all my creative ideas. I thank my friends who truly poured into me and saw these gifts in me. I thank those who made it possible for this book to come to life.

This is my gift to you.

Thank you.

Thank you God!

Introduction

My first Heartbreak

my first heartbreak was something i'll always remember
it would set the tone for the rest of my life
i was young, 10 …yeah 10
4th grade
bright and early on a school day in inglewood, ca
i was still sleeping until i heard it all
a dispute between my mom and my dad
i could hear my mom screaming
i was terrified
i woke up my older brother
my dad had locked the door
i'm not saying it could've been the last time i saw my mom alive
but it could've been
and boom
my mom comes out the door screaming
i never saw my dad this angry until this very morning
it all happened so fast
by the time I knew it …
my dad
the dad that use to drive me in the back of his car till i fell asleep
my dad..
was in handcuffs
they took him to jail
imagine all these events happening in the morning before school
and i still reported to school
no one said anything
not a word
at least a talk to see how i was doing
i wasn't sure how to process my feelings
i was never taught how to
i was young
i was confused
i was floating
i came back home from school
our house was empty
my dad came back and took everything
refrigerator
food
stove
tvs
it was all gone
it was as empty as my heart

this would later turn into a custody battle after they divorced
the two people i loved the most ....hated each other
i was young
i didn't understand why
i had feelings that were never accounted for
this was my first heartbreak
and as I'm writing this
i'm holding back my tears
my heart still breaks 20 years later
again and again

Alexa play Anniversary by Tony Toni Tone

Identity

growing up I never thought I was pretty nor did i think i was ugly
i always thought i was just there
existing
i liked who i was as a person
i was funny
chill and out the way
i loved getting dressed and taking pictures
i had dreams of being a high fashion model
even if we were broke
i made it work for me
at times i did question my beauty
at times i did question the perception other kids had of me
i was not your mixed girl with curly hair
i was the dark/ brown skin girl who always had her hair swooped or those micro braids
i was not the girl that the boys were checking for
especially not in ladera heights, ca
but i never cared
i was comfortable not being seen
but then i became that age where young boys would oversexualize my features
where black kids would assassinate my last name that carried my culture
i didn't get it
i was as black as it got
i remember always running back home and telling my mom
"they keep talking about my lips"
my mom would ALWAYS reassure me
"steph you're so beautiful, do you know that?"
i would immediately feel better
she saw what many would end up seeing later
because i def became a "back then they didn't want me, now im hot, they all on me"
if you know then you know
as an adolescent
i just knew that when i got older i'd get a lip reduction
boy is that like a taboo today
i remember I had a teacher
mr. terry
big
tall
black man
taught history …the audacity
i walked into the school gates
i barely got pass the cafeteria tables

here comes mr. terry
demonstrating clicking sounds as he attempts to call me by my last name
talk about culture appropriation at its finest
but fr self hate
he did this all the time
and normally i'd just ignore him
but this morning i weeped into my english teacher's arms mr. wilkins
mr. wilkins was fine af so it made sense lol
but this morning i had just got yelled at because i left some of my clothes at my dads
dealing with divorced parents was the worst
but when mr. terry lacked the "read the room" autonomy
it was a wrap
when i look back
a grown man tried to strip me of my identity
but little did he know that I had bigger fishes to fry in my life
i was going through alot
showing up to school as normal as i could
was all I could give at the time
but my identity was always going to be something that people lacked maturity for
i was an immigrant
first gen
nigerian- british-american
black girl in a society that would later have to make room for her
i was me

Alexa play Water Get No Enemy By Fela Kuti

Highschool

highschool was the place i thrive as self
i started playing ball
i wasn't the greatest but i had the potential to be the greatest
morningside high school made me think I was going to be a wnba player
my mom hated that lol
i was such an average student
really i just sucked at math
i really did try to apply myself
i just wasn't inspired enough
but ms. ade would change that
ms. ade was my 9th grade biology teacher
nigerian of course
germaphobic …i always think to myself how is she handling covid rn lol
she really was germaphobic af
i mean she would wear gloves to touch our homework assignments
anyways
ms. ade was really mean
she had to be tho
black kids would've walked all over her if she wasn't
but she was less mean to me
i was nigerian
and she knew that
so that softened her up a bit
i was okay being an average student
then ms. ade signed me up for the science fair
i had no intentions to participate
but she knew my mom
i couldn't escape it
i started working on my science project
the science fair came along
i was sooo scared to present my science project in front of faculty
but i pushed through
my mom came
she was so proud of me
that really made me feel good
and I placed
i actually went home with a trophy
the whole time i was operating in my God given talents
but it wasn't about the science fair tho
it was about the opportunity given to me to display my gifts
gifts i didn't even know i had

i made an entire baby fetus by molding playdough with my hands
and created the placenta using a sneaker box
this was the beginning of me understanding how innovative and creative i was
ms. ade believed in me
i didn't even know i was who i was
i spent a lot of my younger years ducked off
it was easier that way
i was never really the type to care for attention
but who i was becoming was going to grabs people's attention anyways

Alexa play Vivrant Thing By Q-Tip

Highschool Part 2

i transferred to a ghetto charter high school
it really was ghetto but it was the best decision my mom could have made
i was mad there was no sports
but there was fashion design
dance
step
etc
Crenshaw Arts Tech Charter Highschool
let's put some respect on it
it was the highschool that saved all the kids in the hood from the hood
catch had the 40's and the 60's
some days were really crazy
i loved fashion design class
it was def my favorite
that was when I first learned about "Dolce & Gabbana" and decided to call myself "STEPHANO"
gabbana's first name is stefano
i just remixed it
i was inspired by fashion
i remember making a collaged spring line
and making my first actual jacket
i felt free at catch
i loved writing poetry for my creative writing class
i learned how to journal too
this would help regulate my emotions
since i was never really taught how to
i got lucky
i remember my first high school boyfriend in 10th grade
kevin brisco
dark skinned
light brown eyes
skateboarder
but rightfully still hood
didn't last that long but i couldn't believe i pulled him
he obviously saw things in me that i couldn't see in myself
catch was where i first watched apocalypto
amazing movie
rudy youngblood was so fine to me
catch gave me a chance to expand on my gifts
ms. pat smith (founder of catch)
she believed in us
all of us
even the gangbangers

she was our mom and grandma at the same damn time
you ever remember getting yelled at then later loved on
that was her
she wanted black kids to win
i forgot to mention my highschool was 98% black
imagine that
one of the most selfless yet driven thing i ever saw ms. pat do
was…
she took 30 black students to the south to look at hbcu's
with her money
i was lucky to be one of them
this would be the first time i ever got on a flight since coming to america when i was 3
we were gone for weeks
she paid for everything
i was so unaware of my blackness outside of being Nigerian
traveling to see all these hbcu's felt like i was finding out more about myself
this trip would forever change my life
to see black people thriving
intelligent
and happy
this was all so new to me
ms. pat showed us we could be more than our circumstances
she was right
i mean we all saw it with our eyes
i came back home knowing that a hbcu was where i belonged
at catch i had a much different identity than i did at morningside
at catch my identity was more in alignment with who i was called to be
there were many like me
personally by the time i got to my senior year
my group of friends were the popular kids
we dressed up as black panthers for halloween
with "free huey" signs
everyone loved that
especially ms.pat
i was surrounded by artists
writers
photographers
dancers
actors
musicians
my group of friends were really the "it' kids
and what made us "it" was our freedom in who we were
i dressed like janelle monae a lot in highschool
i was a good blend of skater chick but make it cute

catch opened my eyes and my heart to my gifts at last

Alexa play Sunshine by Lupe Fiasco

Step Dad From Hell

this was the beginning of a horror story
honestly
the summer before 10th grade
my mom started dating
i remember the first time i saw this nigga
he drove a bronco
red flag out the gate
i knew he wasn't it
can't explain how it all happened so quick but they got married
this man basically moved him and his 3 sons into our 3 bedroom apartment
then we moved from g-block to roxton ave off mlk blvd
by this time I was 5 hours away at college
i missed my mom so much
everytime we got on oovoo I felt this sense of sadness
i knew she wasn't going to tell me
but I just knew something was wrong
after a year away from home
i moved back home for good
everything was fine until his narcissistic true identity started to reveal itself
he would punish my little sister so harshly
she was the youngest
it didn't make sense
it started to cause tension between us and his kids
we moved again
lawndale
honestly who tf just moves to lawndale?
and things got worse
it was out in flesh that he was abusive
if my little sister pissed him off
my mom would suffer the consequences
he was demonic
he would have secret meetings with his sons in the same house
i could tell his goal was to break us all down
i never wanted to run a nigga over so bad and stomp him out
sounds extreme?
if only you knew the things he did
i remember this one specific sunday
he wanted to have a "family" talk which usually he just ends up talking for five hours straight
i wish i was overexaggerating

but i'm not
it's like he loved hearing himself talk
i asked if i could braid my sisters hair while we listened
he of course said no
enemy of progress
i told my mom
she disagreed and explained why she disagreed
before i could fully turn around i could hear the power of the slap
he slapped her
in front of everyone
she yelled and cried
that nearly broke me
it didn't end there
he took a sip of water and tried to spit on us
we dodged it
my mom rebuked it
he called us bastards
that was funny
the fact that he thought name calling was hurtful
especially given the way i felt about my dad anyways
womp womp wompppp
he almost got stabbed that day
which wouldn't be the first time for him
but i wasn't going to let anyone eat those devil's crumbs
he wasn't worth it
he was never worth it to me
he was always pathetic to me
i never said much but i always watched him operate like a maniac
i remember walking into my room with my mom
shutting the door
and i finally found the courage to tell her
"mom we can't do this anymore, we have to leave, i promise we will be alright"
i could see the defeat in her eyes
but i meant it
if it meant i had to get a third and fourth job
i was going to do it
i was already working two part time jobs at the time
it hurt me to see the woman i loved so much be treated like that
by basically a stranger
our house often felt like it was on fire
spiritually
i spent a lot of time just surviving
i barely slept at night because i felt like i needed to be nearby incase my mom needed me
i was always scared that i would wake up one morning and he would've killed her

i lived in fear for almost a decade
i never told a soul what was happening in our household
i suffered for a decade in silence
my mom was precious to me
i didn't want her to feel embarrassed
that's what the nigerian community does
laugh at you when you're down
so i kept it a secret from my friends
i'm really not sure how i operated as normal
deep down i was hurting
but i needed to keep it together for her and my little sister
i was all my mom really had
i was the only one who understood
i was the only one who gave her grace
i never faulted her for making mistakes
she was still a superwoman in my eyes
eventually we got out of there
it almost cost her
her life
he did a lot of terrible things
but you'd be reading this chapter forever if i got into it
to me he was worse than my father
he was the devil in flesh
but one thing he forgot
my mom was a true woman of God
she could never be broken

Alexa play If Heaven Was A Mile Away by Nas Ft. Niky

20 somethings

normally you're supposed to enjoy your early 20's
that wouldn't be my story at all
my early 20's were spent being in my early 40's
make sense?
i was surviving
a lot of people perceived me as nonchalant
but deep down i was functioning through my traumas the best way i could
people wanted so much out of me not knowing how thin i was being spreaded
i saw a lot in my early 20's
celebrated my 21'st in vegas
it was ratchet
saw people do a line of cocaine for the first time ever
hot boxed with some friends and almost got caught at a checkpoint
niggas stole my friends car at a party
was a virgin
niggas treated me special because of that
got pulled over one time because the nigga driving was legit mentally unstable
i thought my life was over a couple of times
almost got jumped by some grown ass women
almost got stabbed on the 40 bus going to mlk
drank a lot of liquor
smoked a lot of weed
my first love broke my heart to pieces
had a crush on the bus driver
almost had a sugar daddy
he was someone i called "uncle"
played truth or dare at the kickbacks
was violated by someone i loved
got my driver's license
was racially tormented in long beach, ca
broke af
half of the time didn't know wth i was doing
was popular in the nigerian community
girls hated me for that
i liked a selective amount of girls
but i really wasn't about that life fr
i was too emotionally unavailable
and it never felt right

but the first and only girl i ever loved committed suicide
that was really tough
her funeral was the first funeral i ever attended
rest in peace _ _ _ _
got kicked out of university
so i came back home and started over
worst feeling ever
i discovered i was a writer fr
well i always knew
i just didn't know it was my gift
so here i was
working everyday monday to sunday
senior in college
writing my first ever script from scratch
i had no backing
i was pulling resources out my ass
basically broke
but i was passionate
i created dangerous waters
a web series that would've put everyone involved on the map
i was so excited about this script that i found a way to almost bring it to life
i casted
i networked
i collaborated
i did it all
until
until someone tried to steal my concept to create their own
this person was apart of the crew
i felt defeated
so i canceled it
i wish people protected me more
i was an artist
and i was sensitive
i was young
with such a huge gift
and niggas really wanted a piece of the pie
i was surprised that i got as far as i did
but people believed in me
believed in the story
i was devastated
i then started a youtube channel
this would become the platform that would cultivate an audience who enjoyed ((me))
youtube was a safe place for me to be myself
just like high school

i created concepts that just came to me naturally
i was having fun
it was the therapy i needed as the trauma and violence was happening behind closed doors
i made it further than i thought i ever would
people doubted how far i would get
that was funny
because yet again
my identity would not be recognized by those around me
here's a story for you
in my early 20's
i went out to a party
i drank a whole lot of liquor
i mixed it all
i was a mess at the party
which was the first and last
so you know i was out bad
i came back home
supposedly the driver slightly hit a pole on the way
thank God i got home safe
i managed to walk up our 5,000 flights of stairs
drunk
made it to my room
then my mom noticed i was drunk
she was shocked because i really wasn't that type of girl
the entire night she slept in the living room and kept an eye on me
in the middle of the night i got up to go to the bathroom
my mom followed me in
next thing you know
i was at the sink
as she held my hair up
while i threw up all this pink liquor
of course i was grounded
but she was always there
i didn't have words back then to express my depression
to express my anger
to express my frustration
i hated our circumstances
i wanted to get out so bad
i wanted to escape
i wanted to die
but i didn't want to disappoint God
how dare i let these gifts go to waste
so i got drunk that night
in hopes that I would feel better

it didn't work
i felt trapped in my early 20’s
i never thought the cycle would end
and even in those spaces
i created
i created opportunities for me to create
my passion would never leave me
it was what helped me get through it all
but I'm not done…

Alexa play Free Mind By Tems

I lost my best friend

this is one of those things
i silently agreed i would take to the grave
but nah
let me crack this open
this would be the first time God gave me decrement
well not the first
but the first of something that felt difficult
like i needed to sacrifice
all i know is i just needed to be obedient
it was beyond my comprehension
my best friend
the only nigga that my mom ever let come over when we lived in lawndale, ca
and the only nigga i didn't mind him coming over to a home that was on fire
we spent a lot of platonic time together but one day shit got real
real in how he felt about me
that was tough
i felt like it was taboo to date him because two years prior i was cool with his ex
there was always this internal battle i experienced
i didn't want people to look at me like that type of girl
because i wasn't
i cared about people's feelings
that's how God made me
but friends would tell me get over it and give him a chance
for a year i would put him through the ups and downs of my emotions
my uncertainty
to be with him
or to not be with him
that was the question
eventually i chose
i may have chose out of pressure
but i wasn't looking back
he was my first
our intimacy was deeper than sex
i was a late bloomer
but retrospectively
a Christian girl
shared a lot of firsts with him
looking back he was a great first
first time i ever felt sexy
and not by his words
but by him allowing me to be free

we rocked for a long while
and then things changed
life threw its jabs as it normally does
and
conviction came
personally he stopped showing up to our relationship
the weight of the world was weighing him down
i didn't know how to deal with that
my world was weighing me down too
but i never missed a beat of our relationship
obviously there were so many other things
but we both were the type to fight for our relationship
especially him
that would change tho
eventually my convictions would become potent
i could hear God telling me that even tho we wanted the same things
we wouldn't be able to achieve them together
we would become exactly like our parents
divorced
i could see it everytime we argued
and i didn't want that
parts of me wanted to escape
escape from him
escape from myself
disappear
vanish
but i knew we loved each other so much
but love was not going to save us
then i did the unfortunate
i broke his heart
i broke it with my lack of language
i broke it with my actions
i broke it with my absence
i didn't know how to tell my best friend that God told me we weren't going to make it
instead i told him everything but the truth
i made up stupid excuses when i knew what was deeply rooted
it ruined everything
it almost ruined him
it almost ruined me
in a perfect world he def deserves an apology for how poorly i went about things
at the time no one spoke about God talking to them
i halfway felt crazy but i knew it was something that had to end
im happy it ended
im happy he found happiness

im happy it all worked out
it was what God intended
i took the bullet
that's what you do for people you love
even if you look crazy

Alexa play Unlawful by La Hara

www.ingramcontent.com/pod-product-compliance
Lightning Source LLC
LaVergne TN
LVHW070210110826
845147LV00002B/552
9798986639604